For our Grannies & Grandpas
those we knew, those long gone
this book is for them all
With Love

Just Abiding

JOE CARPENTER & SON

AN ENGLISH NATIVITY

PERFORMABLE VERSES FOR
CHRISTMAS

BY

Graham Clarke

PHAIDON · OXFORD

PHAIDON UNIVERSE · NEW YORK

Phaidon Press Limited, Musterlin House, Jordan Hill Road, Oxford
OX2 8DP

Phaidon Universe, 381 Park Avenue South, New York, NY 10016

First published 1990
© Phaidon Press Limited 1990
Text, pictures and hand lettering © Graham Clarke 1990

A CIP catalogue record for this book is available from the British
Library

ISBN 0 7148 2676 6

Etchings published by Graham Clarke (Prints) Limited and
distributed worldwide in editions of 400.

Colour and black-and-white illustrations and hand lettering created
by Graham Clarke specially for *Joe Carpenter & Son*.

Designed by Jo Johnson.

Printed in Great Britain by the Roundwood Press Limited, Kineton,
Warwickshire.

PERFORMERS OF THE PIECE

PLAYMASTER   (*The Man in Charge*)

YOUNG JACK SHEPHERD   (*A Shepherd*)

OLD JACK SHEPHERD   (*Another*)

LANDLADY   (*Landlady of 'The Royal Star'*)

JOSEPH   (*A Journeyman Carpenter*)

MARY   (*A Country Girl*)

GABRIEL   (*A Postman Extraordinary*)

HOST OF ANGELS   (*At least 4 Children*)

MELCHIOR   (*A Really Wise Man*)

CASPAR   (*Another*)

BALTHAZAR   (*Yet Another*)

CAMEL DRIVER   (*A Camel Driver*)

LANDLORD OF 'THE ROYAL STAR'   (*A Publican*)

TOM TINKER   (*An 'Egyptian'*)

And did those feet in ancient time
walk upon England's mountains green?

Indeed they did old Billy Blake and
we portray the scene.

THE PIECE

PLAYMASTER. Noble nippers and their nannies,
poorer ones with nice old Grannies;
Cheerful souls and malcontents,
hard working men and gentle gents;
Mums and dads, fat uncles, aunts,
funny visitors from France;
You're truly welcome on this day
to witness this our Christmas play.

Giants, dwarfs and tax collectors,
dustmen, Dukes and bus inspectors;
Soldiers, sailors, tramps and airmen,
even Parish Council chairmen;
Circus clowns with ginger wigs,
nice children fond of guinea-pigs;
You're truly welcome on this day
to witness our fine Christmas play.

Bassoonists who can fly balloons,
balloonists who can play bassoons;
Sainted aunts and second cousins
with relatives by tens and dozens;
Chefs and wizards, saints and crooks,
accountants good at juggling books;
I say you're welcome here today,
please sit and listen to our play.

Gracious ladies, dames and knights,
serfs and squires and troglodytes;
Plumbers, poets, free-lance writers,
amb'lance men and fire-fighters;
Kind men who mend our televisions,
important souls who make decisions;
Come in, sit down, attend I say,
we're about to do our Christmas play.

Country boys who drive great tractors,
psychiatrists and famous actors;
Dinner ladies, queens of beauty,
nice nurses when they're not on duty;
Monks and nuns and holy brothers,
and all those folk who care for others;
Come in, come in, sit down I say,
please enjoy our Christmas play.

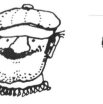

SHEPHERDS Err... 'Scuse me guv'nor, you're in charge?
To us your part seems rather large;
Gabbling as you are up there,
to us it doesn't seem quite fair;
Us shepherds here just keep abiding,
we might as well go into hiding.

This honest agricultural faction
would like to see a bit more action;
Quite likely we'll drop off to sleep,
and hardly need to count our sheep;
Please guv'nor, don't our talents spurn,
we're all set, lets have our turn.

PLAYMASTER Now wait a tick chaps, for I bet
there's someone I've not mentioned yet;
Experts in this field or that,
those who know just where it's at;
Tilers who can shoe a hoof,
and blacksmiths who can tile a roof;
They're all welcome to our play,
on this the very actual day.

Oh I forgot, I feel a fool,
all children from the local school!
Skinny, plump or tall or short,
good at art or keen on sport;
That's my list then, that's the lot,
forgive me if you've been forgot;
You're truly welcome as I say,
witness please our Christmas play.

9

Joe's Place

LANDLORD You're good enough to attend this night,
be patient please, regard our plight,
for none of us is an actor quite;
In our English way we hope to tell
the story you all know so well;
Of how our Jesus, Lord Above,
was born, and God displayed His love.
This sacred tale reflects God's glory,
on the other hand, it's a simple story;
The love of God for me and you
to teach us what is good and true;
The love of Mary for her son,
and the love of Joe for his chosen one;
His task was not an easy one,
to be earthly dad to a heavenly son;
Joe loved his Mary, she loved her Joe
and as true loving people know,
love can mountains overthrow—
with or without the mistletoe.

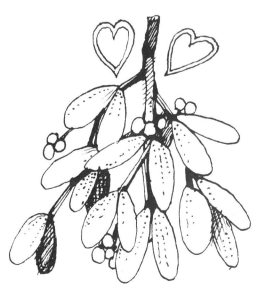

PLAYMASTER.   Now shepherds proceed, let's hear your
                                     views,
  plus any recent farming news.

YOUNG JACK   Jack Shepherd I, a country boy,
  shepherding's my job and joy;
  For I'm their doctor, nurse and friend,
  and to their sheepish natures tend.
  Sheep are prone to coughs and sneezes,
  and complicated sheep diseases
  involving various snorts and wheezes;
  But out on the hills when the North Wind
                              blows,
  stamping about with freezing toes,
  with burning cheeks and dribbling nose,
  delivering lambs in the drifting snows;
  That is when true shepherding shows.

OLD JACK   A shepherd too, see by my smock,
  I love my work and I love my flock;
  My woolly friends rely you see
  on care and kindness from plain old me.
  An ordinary sort of bod
  and yet, to them, I might be God;
  You'll hear Joe Carpenter explain
  that with his hammer, saw and plane
  he can express his dignity;
  Well, so it is with such as me,
  I tell you now I'm proud to be
  a Shepherd for eternity.

PLAYMASTER. Well done good shepherds, that seems fair,
you're really quite a thoughtful pair;
That's put some spirit in this play,
now Joseph, what have you to say?

JOSEPH Well, carpentry's a noble trade
with mallet, chisel, saw and blade;
I call myself a simple bloke
as I deal with ash and elm and oak;
And with my oak and elm and ash
can build a barn or mend a sash;
And using oak and ash and elm
build a boat from prow to helm.
A trade old Noah understood,
though he preferred his gopher wood;
Tenon and mortice fitting true
a first class job is what I do;
All things out of timber made,
cradle to coffin spans my trade;
I'm proud of this my true profession,
and here's an honest self confession:
There's only one thing I love more,
that's my girl, Mary, who lives next door.

MARY   My name kind friends is Mary, an ordinary
                                    name,
no doubt you know of others who are
                 pleased to share the same;
Seldom do we Marys stand out from the
                             crowd,
or boast of our achievements in tones
                     approaching loud,

but on this one occasion (as perhaps you
                          know),
my profile (as they say) was anything but
                            low;
Told by God above to carry out his will,
and thereby ancient prophesies fulfill.

Goodness gracious, a quiet girl like me,
told I'm to be a mother suddenly;
But I hardly could remain unwilling,
when told I was God's word fulfilling.

Chosen from so many others
to be the Holiest of Mothers;
With God's good grace I did come through,
and that's the tale we share with you.

JOSEPH   Betrothed we are but yet to marry,
now you say a child you carry;
I must admit it tests my love,
when you say it's a gift from the Lord
                        above.
But though confused in my emotion,
I give you Mary my true devotion;
My trust in you and yours in me,
will help until we two are three.

Journeyman

PLAYMASTER. Thank you Joseph, that's quite clear,
now what's this object standing here?

GABRIEL   I'm a postman folks, I'll have you know,
I'm proud to work for the G.P.O.;
I'm the messenger in this play,
and I do my postman's job by day.
A bringer of exciting news,
of postcard jokes and seaside views,
bills and letters received with gladness,
and black-edged ones denoting sadness.

I'm not sure you'll believe this quite,
but I'm an Archangel by night,
especially during Xmas seasons;
It's done for economic reasons.
I won't bother with explanation,
or complicate your education;
But thank you for that toleration,
so typical of our English nation.

PLAYMASTER. Have you ever seen the like,
an angel on a postman's bike!
It passes all imagining,
a blessed postman on the wing.

ANGELS   We're angels as from realms of glory,
so vital to this Christmas story;
A marvellous host, a splendid throng,
quite brilliant when it comes to song.

In truth, we're normal boys and girls
beneath these robes and wings and curls;
But no less true in our intent
than cherubs from the firmament.

PLAYMASTER. I imagine you must know
that many, many years ago,
when Romans roamed and Caesar seized,
how conquered nations all were squeezed,
by a system far from fair,
of every ha'penny they could spare;
No excuses were accepted
when Roman poll tax was collected,
and poverty was no protection
in such a stingy tax collection.

GABRIEL Last demand Joe, it can't wait,
attend on this specific date;
Great Augustus back in Rome
decrees, 'Joe you must go back home';
And every Harry, Dick and Tom
to the town where he came from;
Clock in to record more facts
so admin can collect more tax.

PLAYMASTER. So Joseph had to travel back
to place of birth and pay his whack.

JOSEPH Come then Mary, I'm not free
to fight against this new decree;
I think it's best you come with me.

MARY Of course dear Joe, and don't you worry
as long as we don't try to hurry;
We'll take our time along the way,
imagine it's our holiday.

19

PLAYMASTER. So Joe with Mary made a start
with his tradesman's horse and cart.

MELCHIOR. I've gazed at heaven for many a year,
and counted when the night is clear
a million stars both great and small;
I'm pretty sure I know them all.
That brilliant blob there worries me,
I don't know what it is you see;
It's larger than the rest by far,
a real whopper of a star.
Colleagues, really I cannot avoid,
concluding it's an asteroid.

CASPAR. See those shafts of fire spring from it,
that I'm sure is Haley's Comet;
It's brighter than the other lot
by several billion kilowatt;
I'm versed in astronomic arts,
and looking at my maps and charts—
it's stationed over foreign parts.
Do you suppose, friends, at this season,
it's shining for some special reason?

BALTHAZAR. Indeed it is and no mistake,
a lengthy journey we must take,
over the mountains, and if we're able
look for a baby in a stable.
I'm a soothsayer with inside knowledge,
a professor at the Soothsaying College;
I read these signs like an open book,
and this one we can't overlook.
We'll follow this star, unfold this mystery;
What's lying there will soon make history.

The Royal Star

PLAYMASTER. They were the Magi as you've guessed,
I imagine you were quite impressed;
I was myself, I must confess,
it's what they call sagaciousness;
A sage, a wise man, one who thinks,
this next bit though's for kiddlywinks.

CAMEL DRIVER. Though rather awkward looking things,
they're just the job for carrying Kings;
Wise Men and Magi find they're grand
on mud or mountains, grass or sand.
Travelling with speed and grace,
they're hardly just a pretty face;
So useful in so many ways
but 'specially in Nativity Plays.
Not prone to biting, fleas or nits,
distemper, croop or fainting fits;
For King transporting you can't beat a
good old-fashioned Kent three-seater.
With three big humps so soft and comfy,
naturally they're all called … Humphrey.

LANDLORD Landlord of the *Royal Star*,
I stand like a barrel behind my bar;
I keep this alehouse, inn or pub
to serve fine ales and decent grub.
A meeting house for squire and yokel,
I'll have you know we're the favourite local;
Where patrons, keen on bar room arts,
play crib or dominoes or darts.

LANDLADY For me, kind friends, as the Landlord's wife
this is not what you call the quiet life;
The busiest we've ever been,
a noisier lot I've seldom seen;
I've not had time to make a pudd'n
this Christmas, though I make a good'n.
That Caesar and his Roman army
could well drive us landladies barmy;
With all the coming and the going,
at census time there is no knowing
how many folk are like to tread
steps to our door to seek a bed.

LANDLORD Both regulars and travellers weary,
though perhaps I'm mildly beery,
will find me jolly, brisk and cheery;
At every client's beck and call,
I remain, with luck, a friend to all.
But at this moment we've to cope
with this so called census. So let's hope
no extra lodgers give a knock,
in fact I think I'll turn the lock.
Ah! What's that noise outside? I fear
one more is seeking lodgings here;
Look here, good Sir, I will unlock
but we're absolutely chock-a-block.
No room old pal, I'm sorry mate,
I'm afraid you've left it rather late.

Look Wot's Arrived

PLAYMASTER. Joseph whispers man to man,
'Please help my Mary if you can';
He tells the nature of his plea
and underlines its urgency.

LANDLORD Oh Lord, a proper problem this is,
I think I'll go and fetch the missus.

LANDLADY Husband stand aside I say,
get your fat body out the way.

PLAYMASTER. She's seen this kind of thing before
and greets poor Mary at the door.

LANDLADY Forgive me dear for my suspecting;
Am I correct? You are expecting?
Yes, of course dear and I vow
your time is any moment now.
Now look here dear please don't give in,
it's true we've no space at the inn;
Proper bedrooms we might lack,
but we've this stable round the back;
Quite cosy really, not too large
and you can have it free of charge.
Expert motherly advice I'll lend,
don't worry dear, you've found a friend.

PLAYMASTER. According to our testament
in that crude place, the night they spent;
And thus God's greatest gift was sent
and all the world for all these years has seen
birth as a Sacrament.

ANGELS All people cares aside are flinging,
let hope in tired hearts be springing,
just listen to our heavenly singing;
With joyful sounds we'll fill the sky,
and trained especially up on high,
not only sing but really fly
on wings fixed on with strong elastic
do aerobatics quite fantastic;
Let angels be your inspiration,
let dancers dance in celebration,
let bells ring out across this nation,
It's Christmas: time of jubilation.

SHEPHERDS Old King David was a shepherd too,
zonked Goliath with that stone he threw;
Our man Dave sure did his thing
with a little round pebble and his deadly
sling.
No wayward sheep could come to harm,
while he composed another Psalm;
The rolling stones that singer slung
were great whether spoken or simply sung.
A likely lad but a great King too,
a hero both for me and you.

PLAYMASTER No wonder God made his selection
from the very same direction;
God grant all shepherds his protection.

Stable Lad

OLD JACK   Bold as us shepherds might appear,
I'm nervy at this time of year;
Maybe you think I'm weak and silly,
but when it's dark and damp and chilly
I fancy there are wolves about,
with grizzled gob and snappy snout
ready to snatch a sheep or lamb.
There! I'm frightening myself, I am.

YOUNG JACK   On such dark nights and at this season,
it's possible to lose one's reason.

OLD JACK   Especially when the wind is blowing
and worse, if suddenly it's snowing;
Oh goodness me the sky is glowing!

YOUNG JACK   Hark! What's that sound? The dark is
lightening.
Sweet music! But it's rather frightening.
What's that object shining bright?
D'you think perhaps a meteorite?
If it is, it's stopped in flight;
Is this some special sort of night?

OLD JACK   I think, young chap, you could be right;
A host of angels in the skies?
To me, son, this is no surprise;
I'm certain that this heavenly choir
announces the birth of our Messiah!

PLAYMASTER   Ideas the Great Jehovah's planned,
that over some millennia spanned,
are sung of by our angels' band.

ANGELS   Brave shepherds hear our song of love
          for you and everyone;
          Our great forgiving Lord above
          sends mortal men his Son;
          We sing now of the Saviour's birth,
          such wondrous news we bring
          The heavenly child down here on earth.
          Go shepherds seek your King.

YOUNG JACK   The King that we've so long awaited?
              The Messiah the Holy Bible stated
              would be the Saviour of our land
              to break the cruel oppressor's hand?
              Is this the actual culmination
              of hopes for our most troubled nation?

Ye Faithful

OLD JACK That star's our signal I'll be bound,
beneath it will our King be found,
as prophesied by old Isaiah.
Let's up and away! Stamp out the fire!

YOUNG JACK This startling message makes things seem
as though this night is just a dream;
Why us old man?; Why should we be
called to meet Royal company?

OLD JACK Why not, young lad? Our hearts are true,
we're decent chaps, both me and you.

YOUNG JACK But don't you fear while we're away
that there's a chance our sheep might stray?

OLD JACK I doubt it with that star so bright,
just now it's more like noon than night;
Don't dream up things so problematical,
folk will think you're sheepdogmatical.

YOUNG JACK O.K., I'll brighten up as since
we're off to meet this Royal Prince;
Maybe, old man, we're simple peasants,
that doesn't mean we can't take presents.
Give me your crook, I'll catch a lamb,
I'm in the party mood, I am.
Come on then dad, look sharp I say,
this feels to me like Christmas day!

PLAYMASTER. So our shepherds left their sheep
who no doubt had a good night's sleep;
No chance of nasty wolves that night
as old Jack said, 'far too much light';
They left the hills and travelled down
to seek their Saviour in the town.

MARY Well here am I, a mother now;
This stable, my delivering place;
The lamb with sheep, the calf with cow;
To give birth here was no disgrace.

Such creatures' presence make me sure
as I look around the stable's gloom;
It's natural, simple, good and pure.
For me, this was the perfect room.

Sweet grasses strewn upon the floor,
my baby sleeps and so does Joe;
But early daylight's at the door
And soon no doubt the cock will crow.

A Holy Mother, earthly wife;
The rooster crows, and there's the warning
that was the great night of my life.
Wake up Joe, it's Christmas morning!

JOSEPH Mary, you've filled my heart with joy
producing such a fine young lad;
He's such a sturdy little boy
he'll be a tradesman, like his dad.

He'll help me in my daily task;
Dear Mary, teach him to be good,
to sweep up shavings when I ask,
and I'll teach him to work with wood.

When his apprenticeship is done,
all made to measure and bespoke,
we'll be Joe Carpenter and Son,
craftsmen in fine English oak.

MELCHIOR.	Good evening all, we're in Judea— must call on Herod while we're here.
CASPAR.	Tea and a chat, that's our intention, a rather nice polite convention.
MELCHIOR.	We visiting Wise Men can't neglect to show that monarch due respect.
BALTHAZAR.	We'll tell our story so that he can tell us where our King might be. He's bound to know; he's royalty.
PLAYMASTER.	Not realising what's in store our Magi tap upon the door; A swanky servant shows them to his master's royal rendez-vous; Herod blasts them with his views on various aspects of the news; But when he hears the Magi's quest drops his fag-ash down his vest; He's most suspicious then and sly and has a slightly drooping eye. Not being offered any tea, out come our wise men, one, two, three.
MELCHIOR.	Phew! Hardly what you call Prince Charming, I found his manners quite alarming; I'm sorry now that we let slip the actual purpose of our trip.

40

Realm of Glory

CASPAR. Did you notice his cruel eyes,
'How very nice'?, he's telling lies;
News of our search was a surprise,
you bet your boots he'll send out spies.

BALTHAZAR. I'm sad we told him anything,
he's quite unfit to be a King;
Normally I'd put a curse on
such a ghastly type of person.

PLAYMASTER. Our Wise Men being awfully wise
once again looked to the skies,
saw their star much brighter yet
and at its light their sights they set;
Over hedge and ditch and stile,
ever onwards, mile on mile,
till at last they found their prize,
and though diminutive in size,
God spoke to them through baby's eyes.

MELCHIOR. Gold is costly, precious, yellow,
not suited to your humble fellow;
Golden Gold, the sign of Kings,
of crowns and orbs, Imperial things.
But it's pure and solid, good and true,
here little King—my gift for you.

CASPAR.   Frankincense I do present
so reverence is my intent;
A holy token of devotion
invoking joy and sweet emotion.
Accept this gift with sacred smell
and take my heart and soul as well.

BALTHAZAR.   Myrrh, gift of sorrow, I do give.
This sign of sadness please forgive,
but prophets wondrous words have spoken,
so I acknowledge with this token.
He will be Great. The Messiah maybe …
a prophetic sign for your little baby.

PLAYMASTER.   Our Magi, done with adoration,
retreat to nearby camel station;
Exhausted by the day's events,
they have a kip inside their tents;
Later just as day was dawning,
Gabriel gave his famous warning:

GABRIEL 'O Honoured Magi, wise and grand
don't call on Herod on your way;
We'd like to change the route you've
                                    planned,
make visiting another day.
We know he asked you to call in,
with seeming interest in your mission,
his motive though is black as sin,
so treat that man with great suspicion.
Your Royal quest made Herod fear
a change of monarchs in Judea.
If you please gents, don't go near;
This sound advice is Heaven sent,
good Wise Men, Herod circumvent!

MELCHIOR Good gracious, colleagues what a fright,
an awesome message in the night.

CASPAR This proves our notions on that King,
his nastiness and everything.

BALTHAZAR Let's nip off home without a call
not see his horrid face at all.

ALL THREE MAGI When he finds out we haven't called,
he'll tear his hair out, 'cept he's bald.
Forget old Herod, let's depart
with young King Jesus in our heart.

Inglenookers

GABRIEL Joseph! A message from above:
Take that baby you so love,
put him and Mary in your cart,
and hit the road, buzz off, depart!
That Herod, tyrant of this land,
a beastly massacre has planned;
He's sinful, spiteful, cruel and bad,
so envious, he's almost mad.
Your precious lad's in mortal danger,
seek refuge with some friendly stranger;
Away, away, go way down South,
take it from this horse's mouth.

PLAYMASTER That's the style of Herod's scheming,
don't doubt it, just because you're dreaming.

JOSEPH   Pack our cases, find his toys!
King Horrid's out to murder boys!
A dreadful nightmare! Oh, I bet
it was that chunk of cheese I ate;
I'll not take chances though, not me,
not with a monster such as he;
Come Mary, grab the boy, let's flee!
From Angel Gabriel's description
I think we're going to go Egyptian;
That raving tyrant must be mad
trying to kill our little lad.

PLAYMASTER.   So once again they made a start
in Joseph's little tradesman's cart.

TOM TINKER. Tom Tinker I, a travelling man,
I journey this land over;
I wander the lanes with my horse and van,
I'm called the Gypsy Rover.
I cut straight willows by the stream
for pegs and basket weaving;
Of pastures new I then will dream,
up sticks, and soon be leaving.

I brew strong tea in an old black can
and weave the willow basket;
I'll mend you a kettle, pot or pan.
Address? Well please don't ask it.
Oft' times as might seem opportune,
at night it is my habit
to creep beneath the midnight moon
to bag a fowl or rabbit.

Should Joe stranger happen by,
I care not saint or sinner;
Him I'll ask and be not shy
to share with me my dinner.
To sit around the rag-stone hearth
with company's my pleasure;
The friends I make along this path
bring joys that know no measure.

PLAYMASTER. Then suddenly one joyous day,
a man jumped off his bike to say:

Tom Tinker

GABRIEL Mary! Baby! Old friend Joe!
I'm not just here to say hello;
This message that I now impart
will stir your soul and warm your heart;
King Herod, nastiness himself,
has had his crown put on the shelf;
That murderous object of disgust
is dead, a gonner, bit the dust.
He's snuffed it, folks, his time is passed,
you can go back home at last.

PLAYMASTER Hooray! Hooray! For what came next
I recommend another text;
Read sometime soon the follow on
by Matthew, Mark and Luke and John.

LANDLADY Our carpenter, young son of Joe
grew up with fisherfolk, and then
became a preacher as we know,
and so a fisherman of men;
'Love your God', said Jesus preaching,
'the key to joy you there shall find;
Follow then my second teaching
and share your love with all mankind.'

PLAYMASTER Thus ends our play this winter night,
we trust it met with your delight;
Forgive us please the weaker parts,
doubt not the truth though of our hearts;
Through simple souls and simple arts,
sometimes Great God His truth imparts;
May Father, Holy Spirit, Son,
this Christmas bless us every one.

ALL
Quiet rows of faithful kneeling
praising God for Christmas time;
Then the festive rounds are pealing
all village England's church bells chime.

Tread the path from church or chapel,
see smoke from cottage chimneys climb;
That fine fat goose well stuffed with apple
will celebrate this Christmas time.

Gather for the Christmas feast
that brightens England's winter clime;
From the greatest to the least
give thanks to God it's Christmas time.

Crowd around the cheering barrel,
dear children play your pantomime;
Chant loud and long this joyful carol
with all your hearts—it's Christmas time!

A true wise man might play the fool
for foolishness might well be wise;
The fool who breaks the wisest rule
might wisely open foolish eyes.

The End
and the Beginning